Want free goodies?
Email us at freebies@pbleu.com

@papeteriebleu

Papeterie Bleu

Shop our other books at
www.pbleu.com

Wholesale distribution through Ingram Content Group
www.ingramcontent.com/publishers/distribution/wholesale

For questions and customer service, email us at
support@pbleu.com

FREE PDF DOWNLOAD OF THIS BOOK

www.pbleu.com/financelife

YOUR DOWNLOAD CODE: FNC373

 @papeteriebleu

 Papeterie Bleu

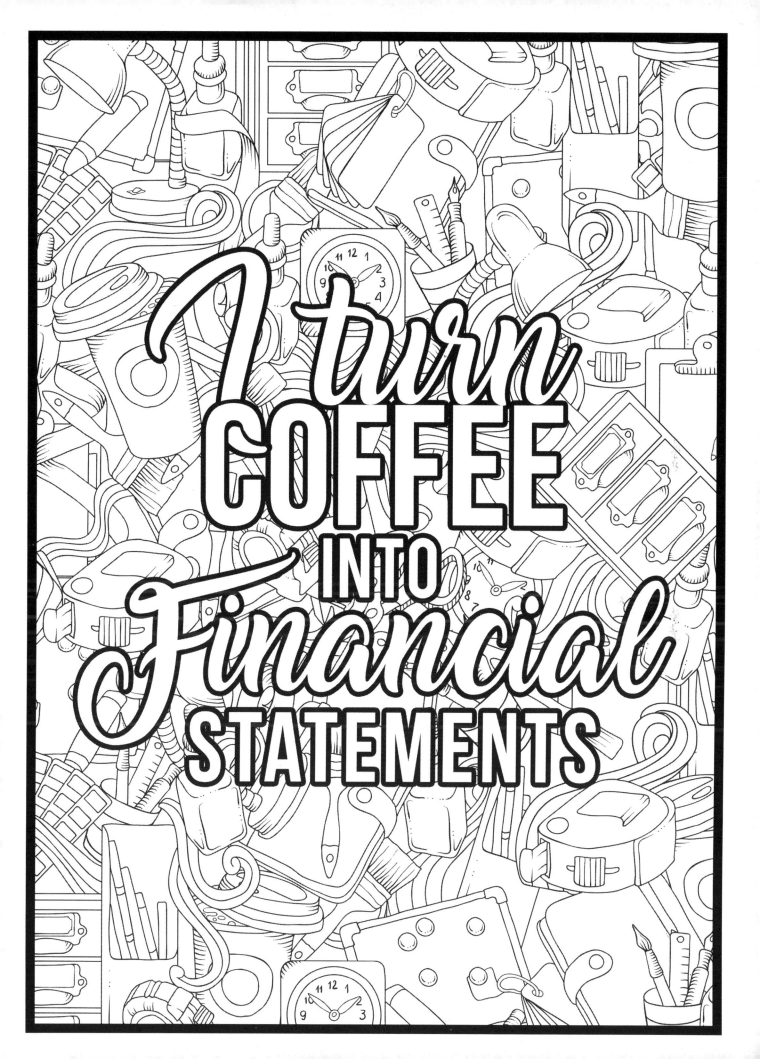

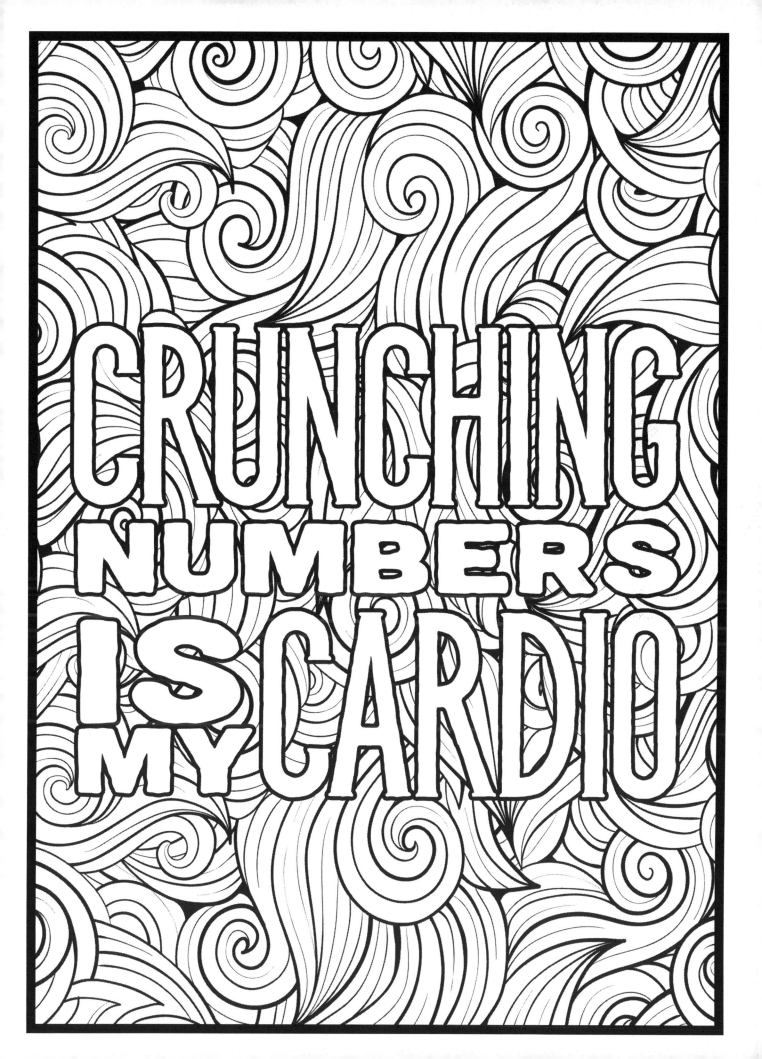

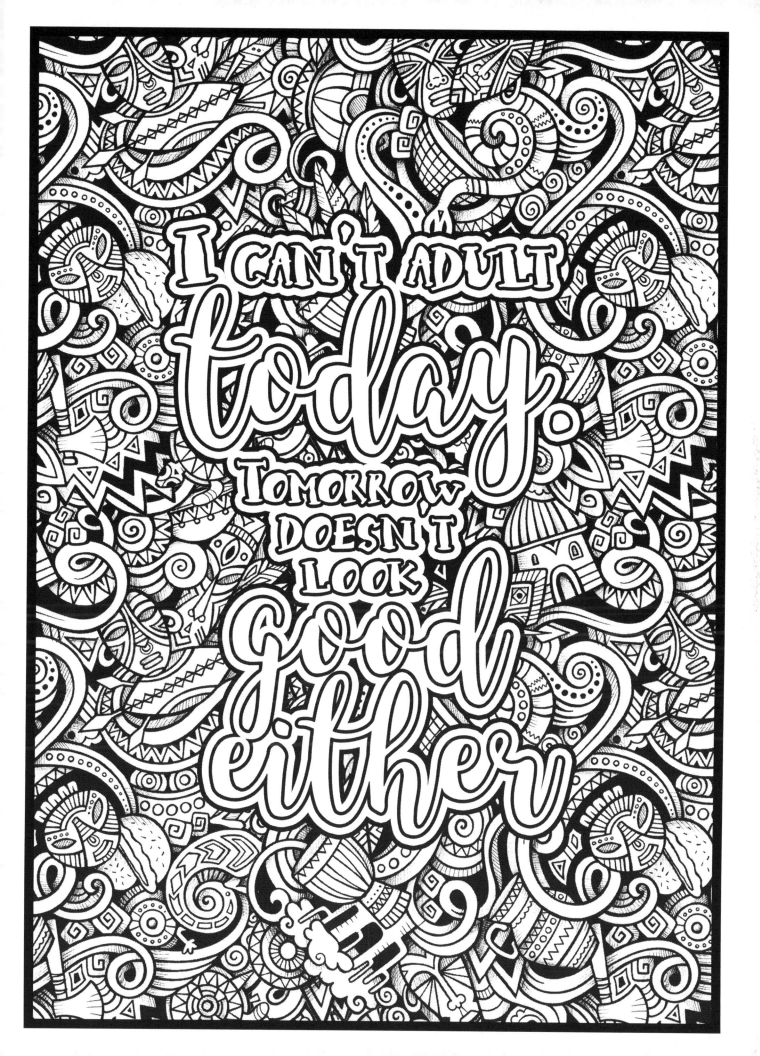

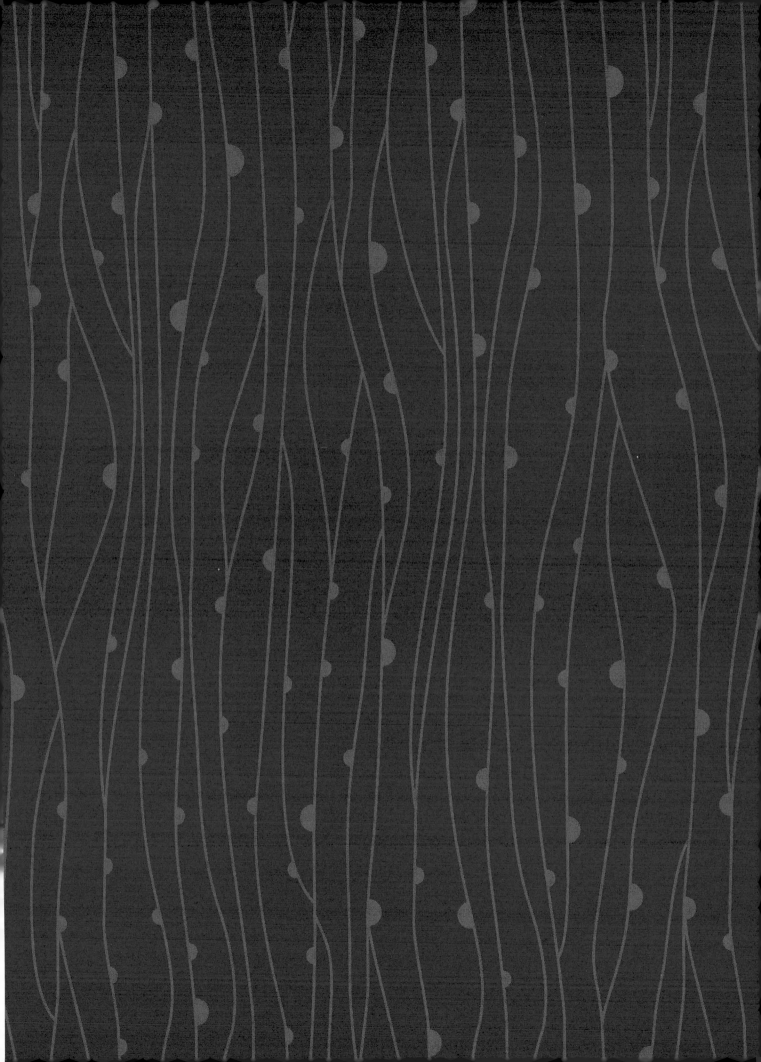

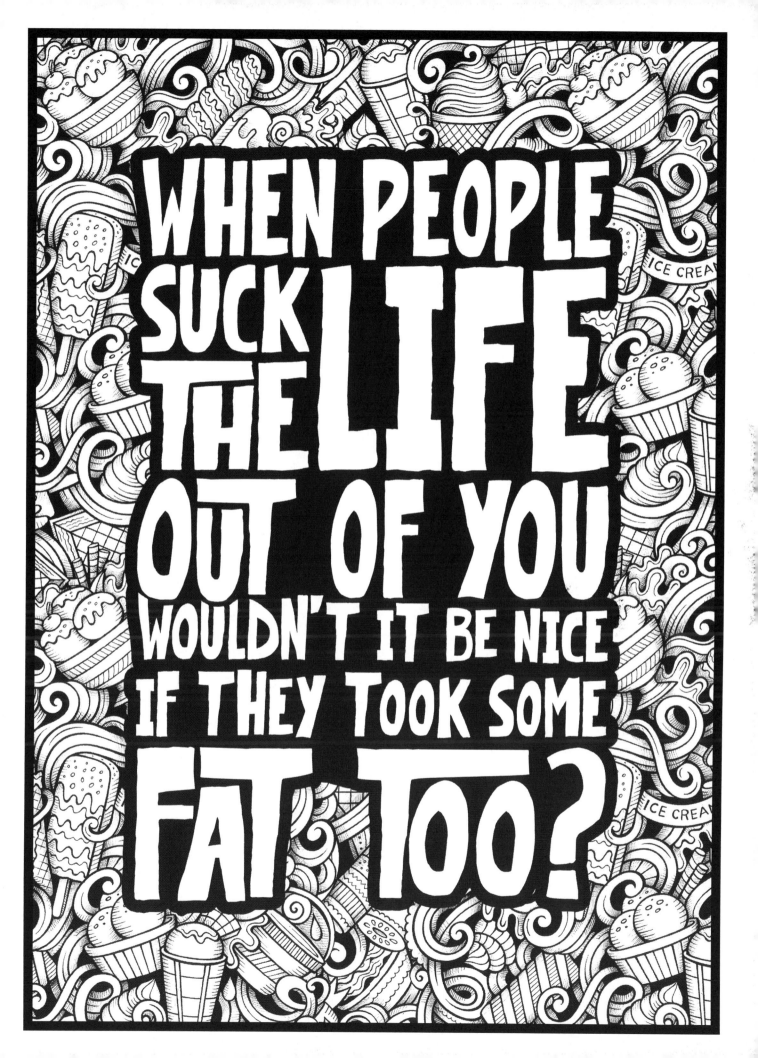

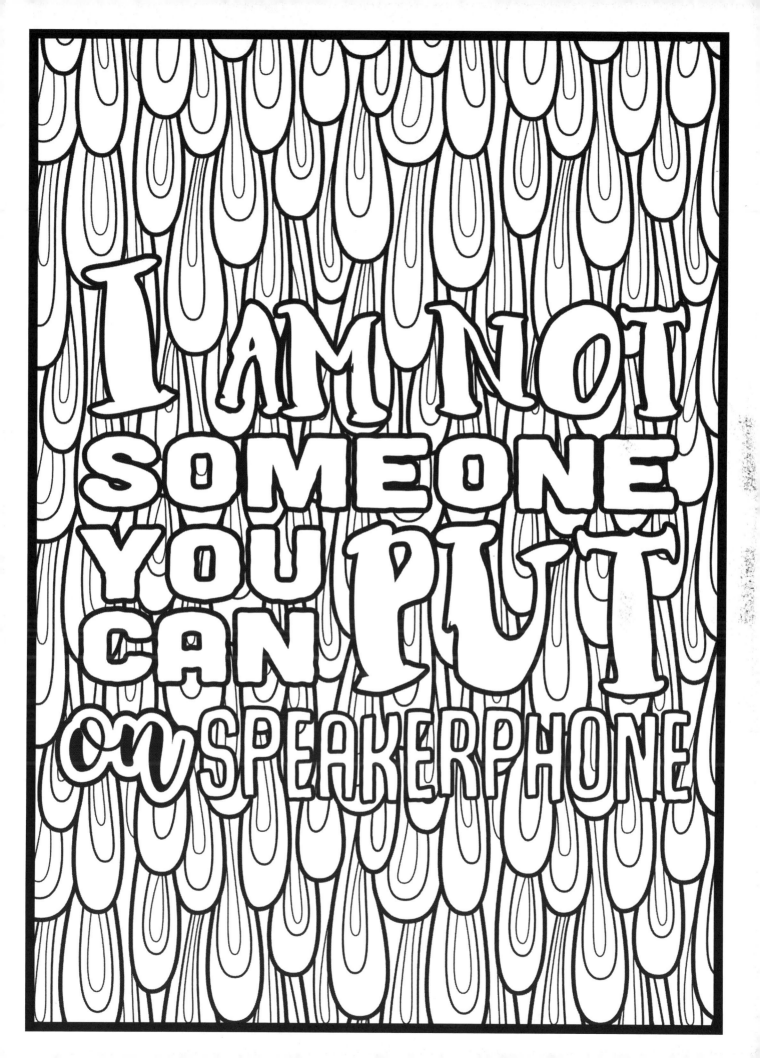

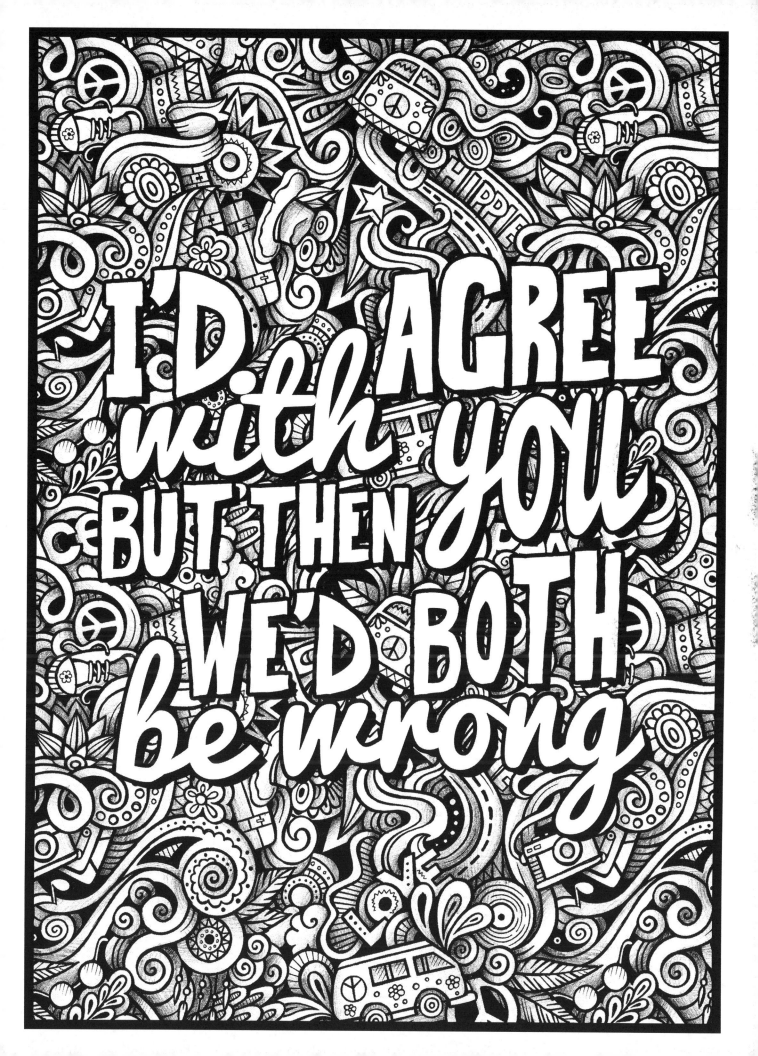

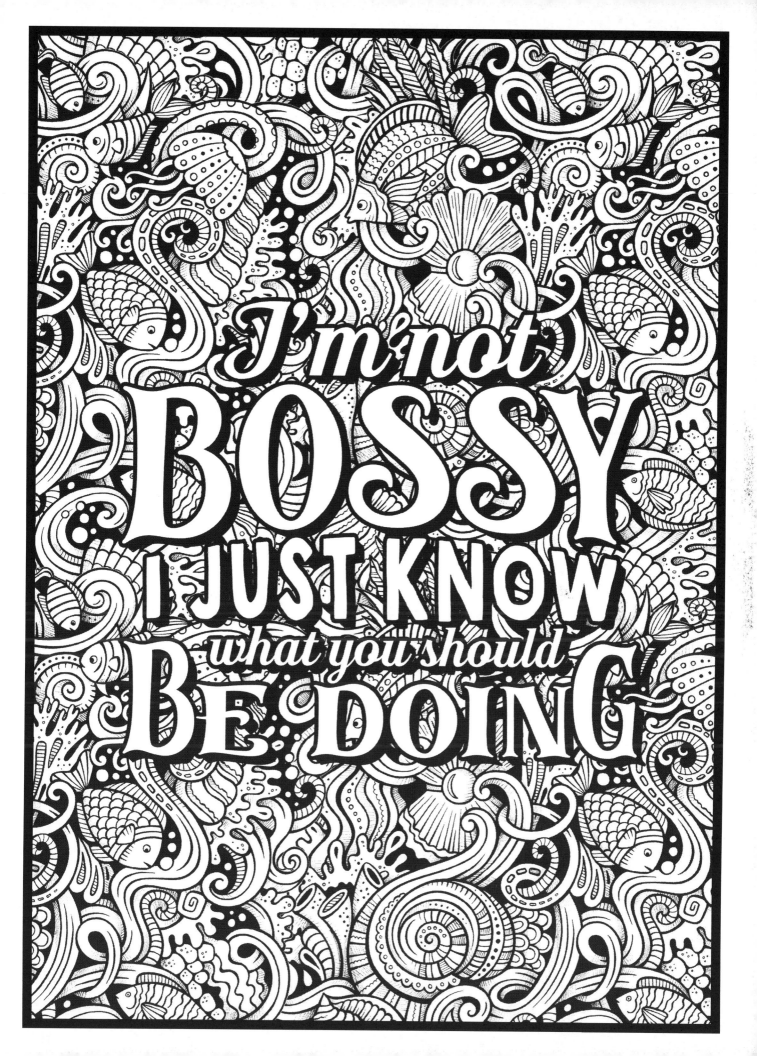

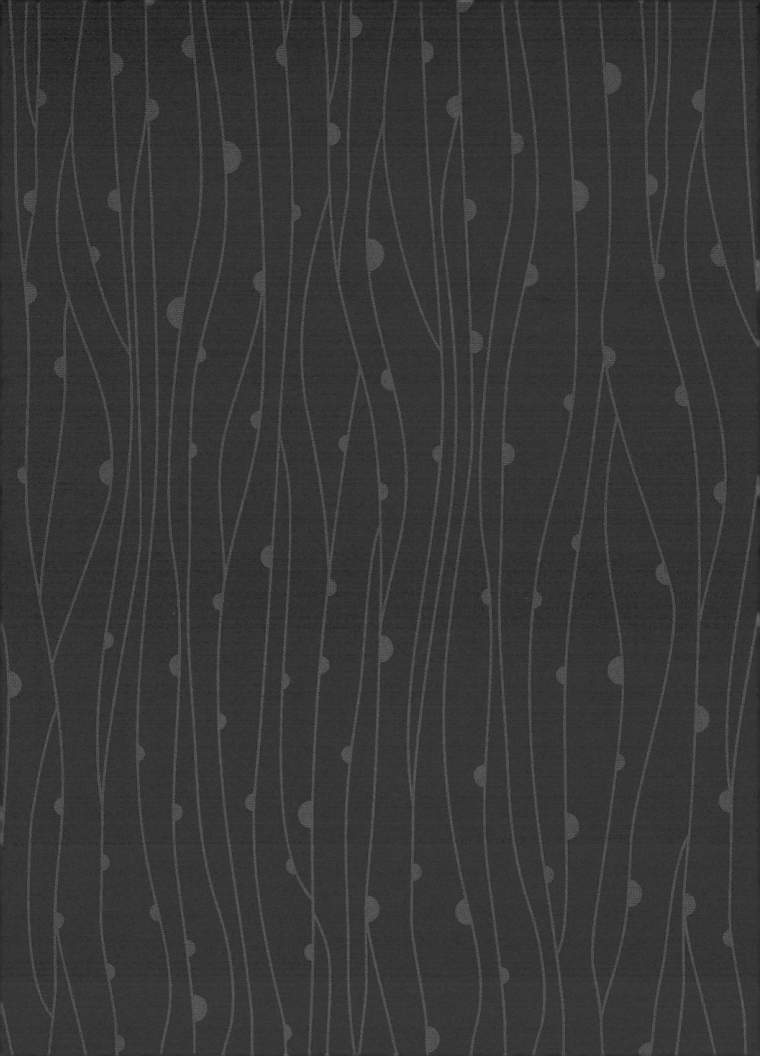

Happiness is not Having to SET an alarm for TOMORROW

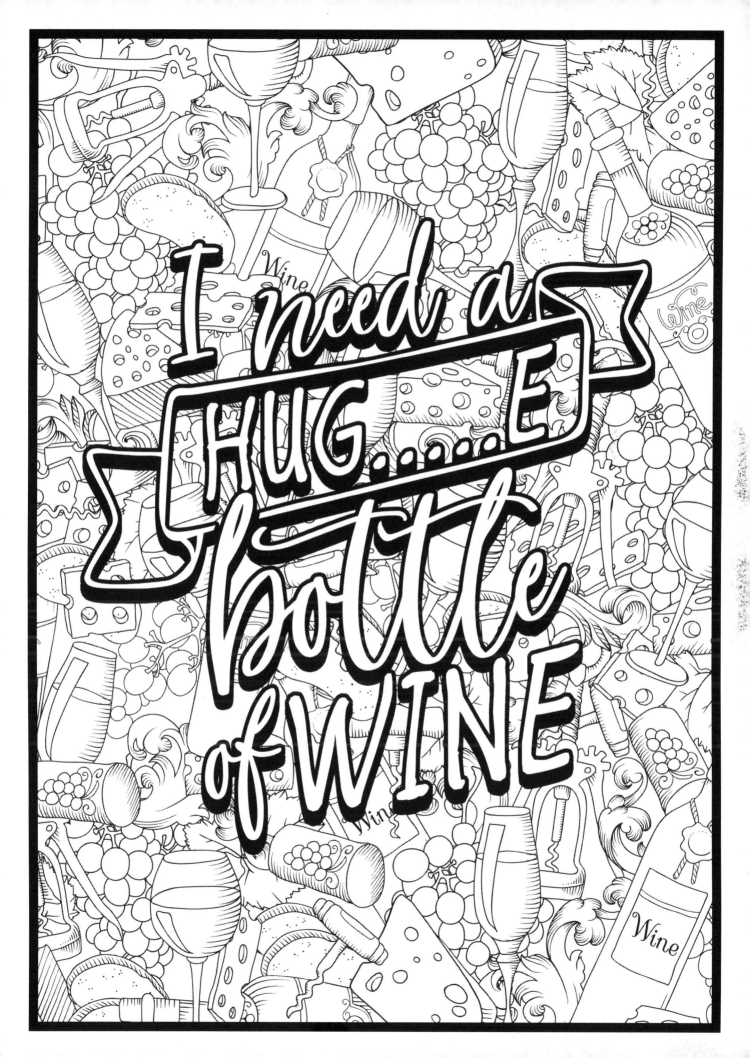

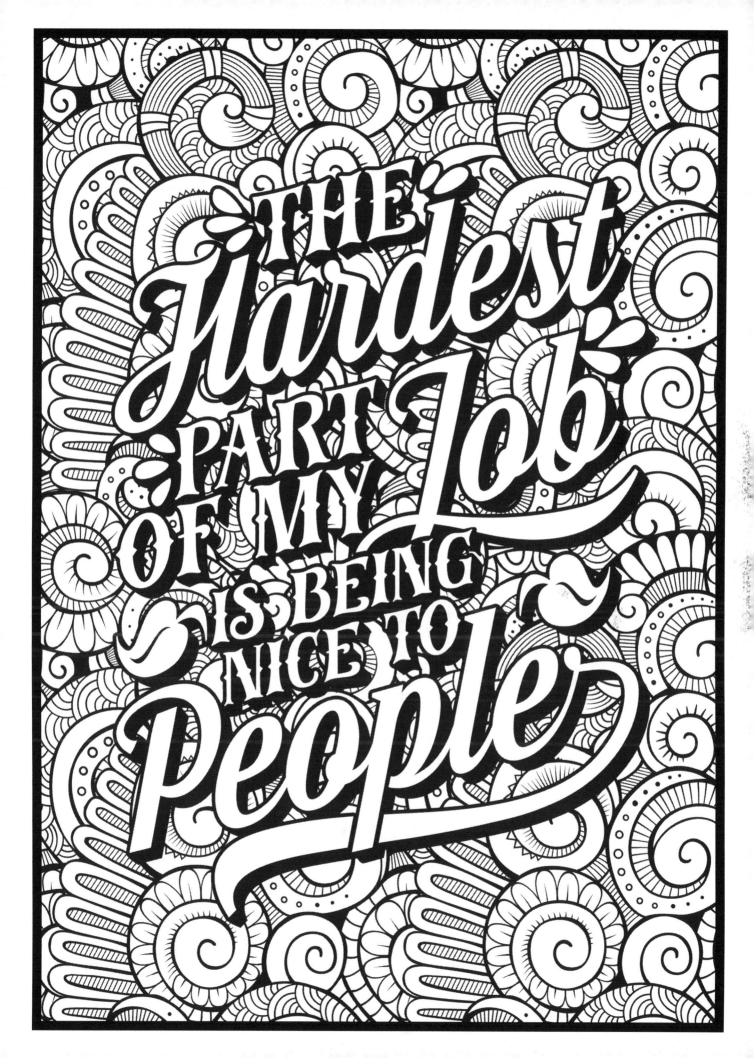

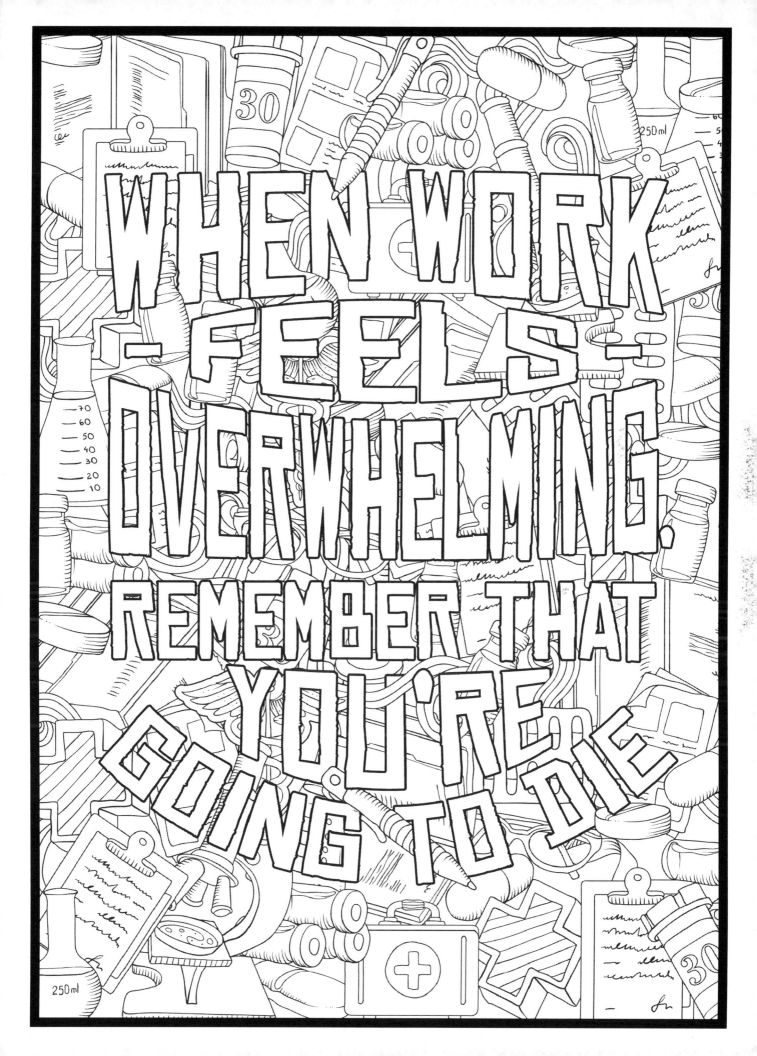

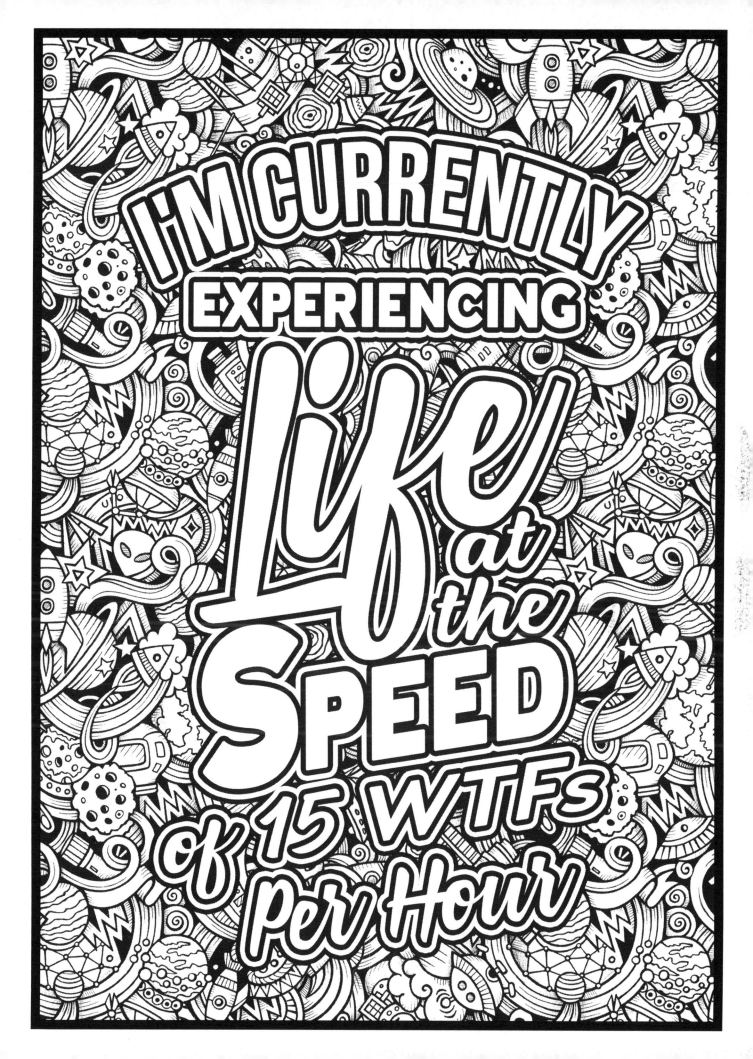

I'VE SEEN MONKEY FECES FIGHTS AT THE ZOO MORE Organized THAN MY WORKPLACE!

My Goodness that sounds
like a BIG mess sir.
UNFORTUNATELY
I
just
Realized
that
I Quit.
GOOD LUCK
with that.

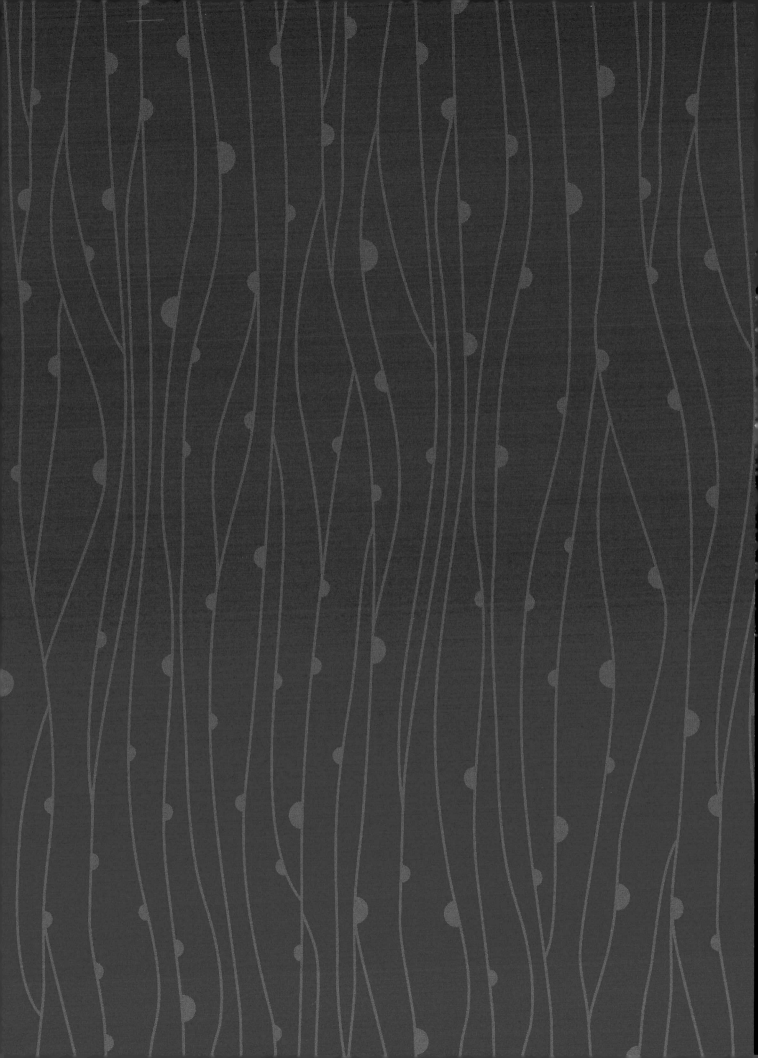

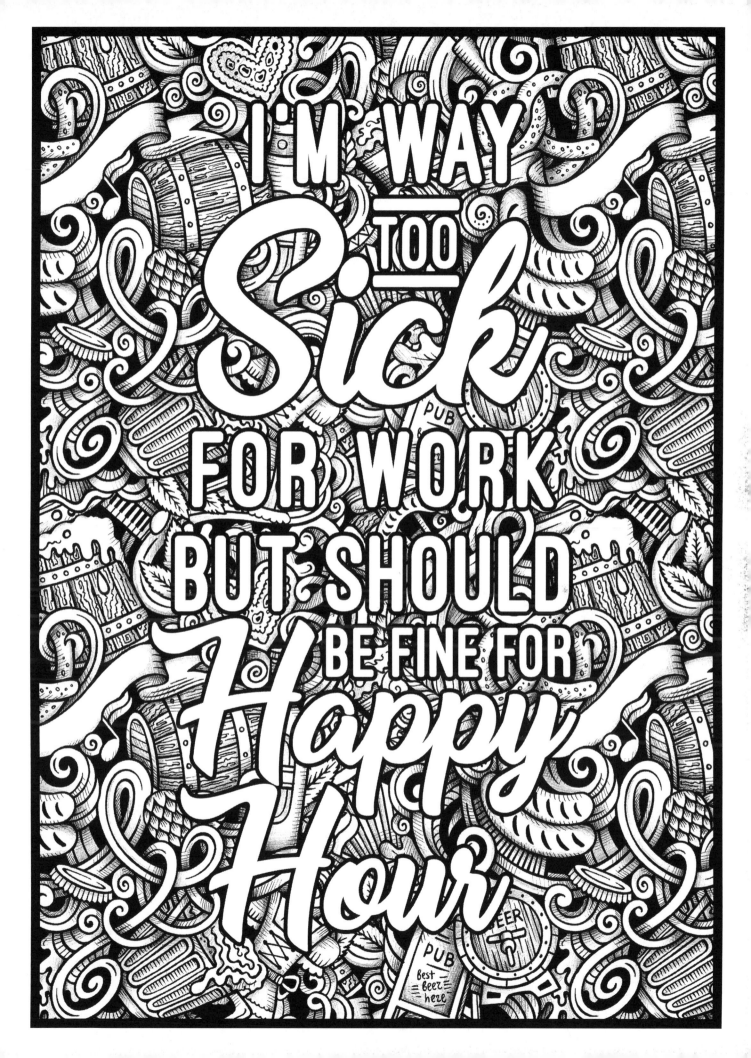

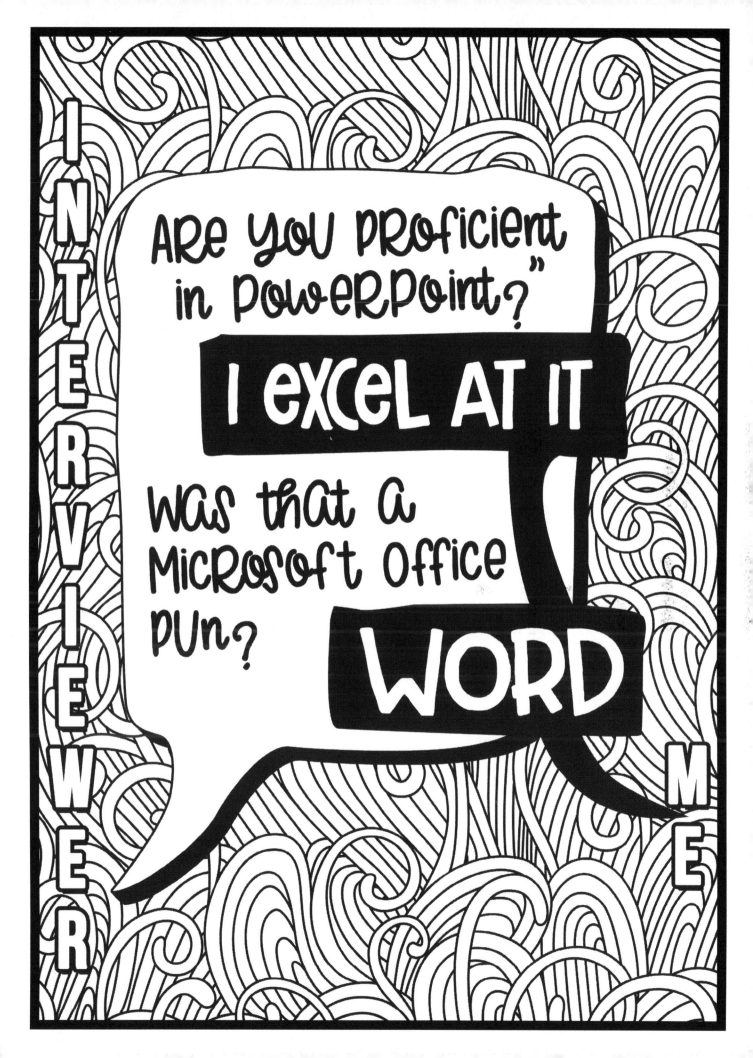

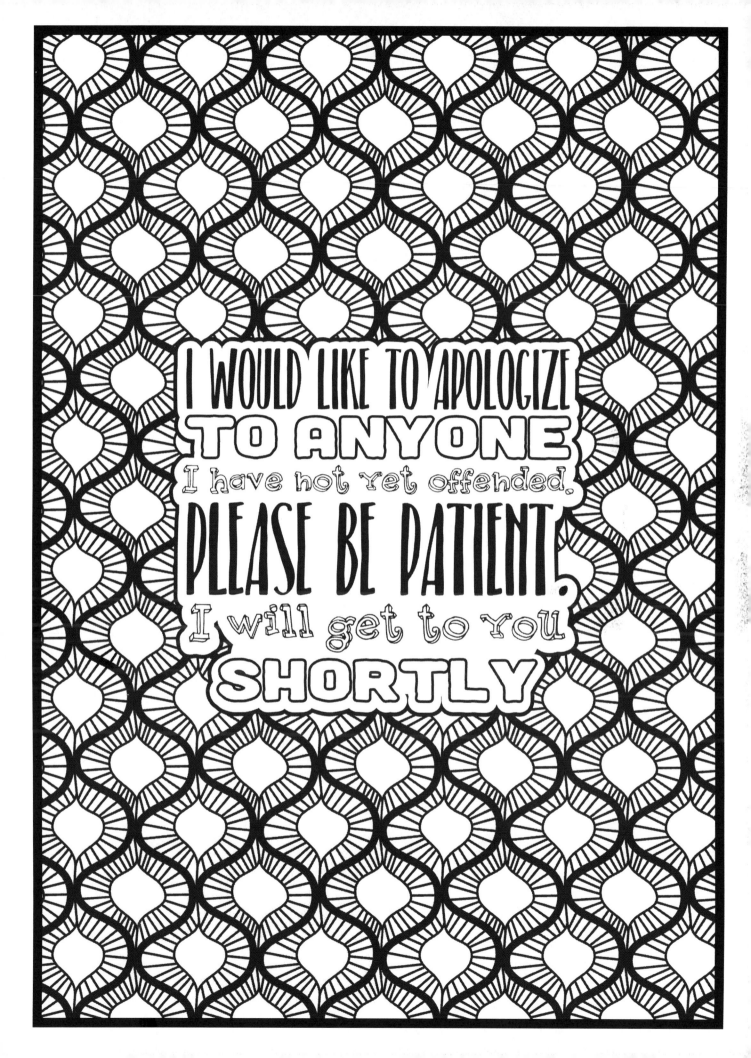

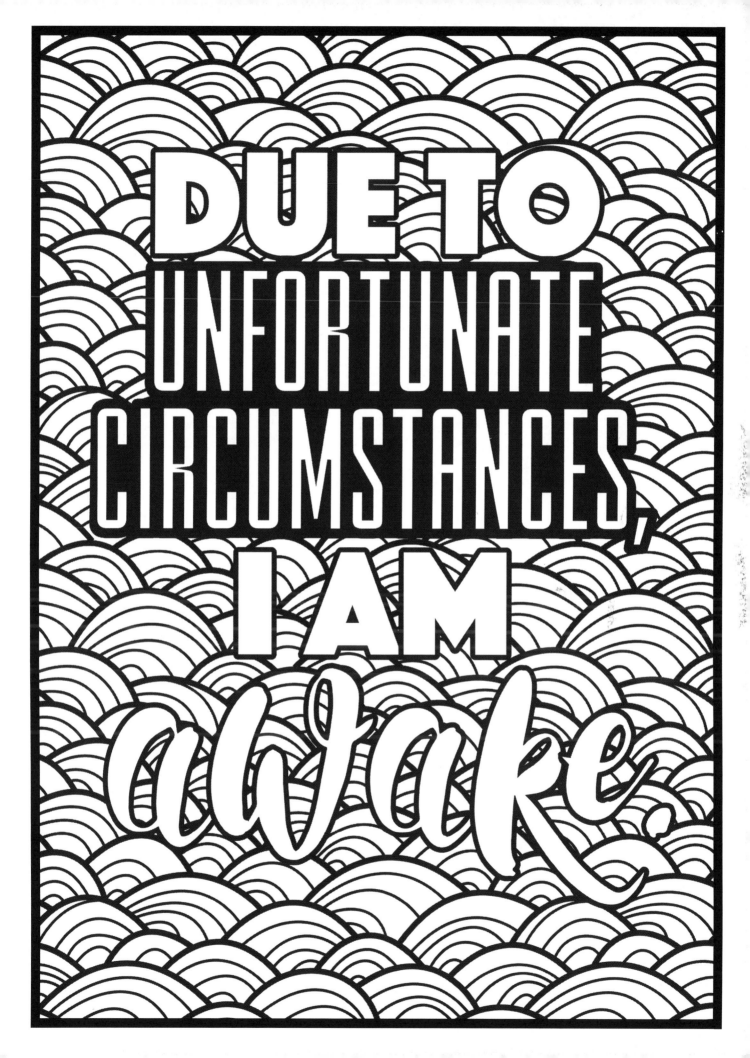

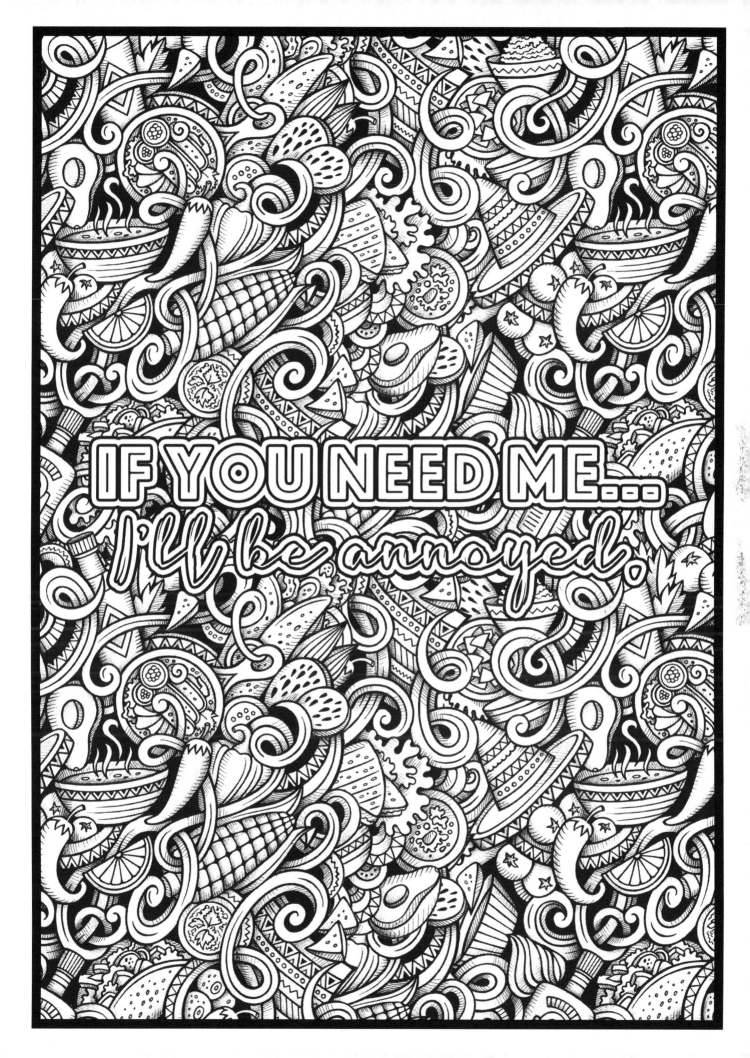

FREE PDF DOWNLOAD
OF THIS BOOK

www.pbleu.com/financelife

YOUR DOWNLOAD CODE: FNC373

 @papeteriebleu

 Papeterie Bleu

Want free goodies?
Email us at freebies@pbleu.com

@papeteriebleu

Papeterie Bleu

Shop our other books at
www.pbleu.com

Wholesale distribution through Ingram Content Group
www.ingramcontent.com/publishers/distribution/wholesale

For questions and customer service, email us at
support@pbleu.com

Made in the USA
Columbia, SC
12 June 2020